Master Maths at Home

Geometry and Shape

Scan the QR code to help
your child's learning at home.

mastermathsathome.com

How to use this book

Maths — No Problem! created Master Maths at Home to help children develop fluency in the subject and a rich understanding of core concepts.

Key features of the Master Maths at Home books include:

- Carefully designed lessons that provide structure, but also allow flexibility in how they're used.

- Speech bubbles containing content designed to spark diverse conversations, with many discussion points that don't have obvious 'right' or 'wrong' answers.

- Rich illustrations that will guide children to a discussion of shapes and units of measurement, allowing them to make connections to the wider world around them.

- Exercises that allow a flexible approach and can be adapted to suit any child's cognitive or functional ability.

- Clearly laid-out pages that encourage children to practise a range of higher-order skills.

- A community of friendly and relatable characters who introduce each lesson and come along as your child progresses through the series.

You can see more guidance on how to use these books at **mastermathsathome.com**.

We're excited to share all the ways you can learn maths!

Copyright © 2022 Maths — No Problem!

Maths — No Problem!
mastermathsathome.com
www.mathsnoproblem.com
hello@mathsnoproblem.com

First published in Great Britain in 2022 by
Dorling Kindersley Limited
One Embassy Gardens, 8 Viaduct Gardens, London SW11 7BW
A Penguin Random House Company

The authorised representative in the EEA is Dorling Kindersley
Verlag GmbH. Amulfstr. 124, 80636 Munich, Germany

10 9 8 7 6 5 4 3 2 1
001–327094–Jan/22

A CIP catalogue record for this book is available from the British Library.

ISBN: 978-0-24153-939-2
Printed and bound in the UK

For the curious
www.dk.com

MIX
Paper from
responsible sources
FSC™ C018179

This book was made with Forest Stewardship Council™ certified paper - one small step in DK's commitment to a sustainable future. For more information go to www. dk.com/our-green-pledge

Acknowledgements
The publisher would like to thank the authors and consultants Andy Psarianos, Judy Hornigold, Adam Gifford and Dr Anne Hermanson.

The Castledown typeface has been used with permission from the Colophon Foundry.

Contents

	Page
Measuring the surface that a shape covers	4
Measuring area by counting squares	6
Measuring area and perimeter	8
Measuring area by multiplying	10
Measuring area using squares and triangles	12
Measuring area using grid lines	14
Knowing types of angles	16
Comparing angles	18
Classifying triangles	20
Classifying quadrilaterals	22
Identifying symmetrical figures	24
Drawing lines of symmetry	26
Making symmetrical figures	28
Completing symmetrical figures	30
Describing position on a 2D grid	32
Describing position using coordinates	34
Plotting points	36
Describing position after translation	38
Describing movement	40
Review and challenge	42
Answers	46

Ruby   Elliott   Amira   Charles   Lulu   Sam   Oak   Holly   Ravi   Emma   Jacob   Hannah

Measuring the surface that a shape covers

Starter

How many squares does Holly need to cover the surface of the picture?

Example

The total surface of the picture is called its area.

Holly needs 12 squares to cover the surface of the picture.

Measure and cut out some 2-cm squares from a piece of card.
You can use a cereal packet for the card.
How many squares do you need to cover the surface of each shape?

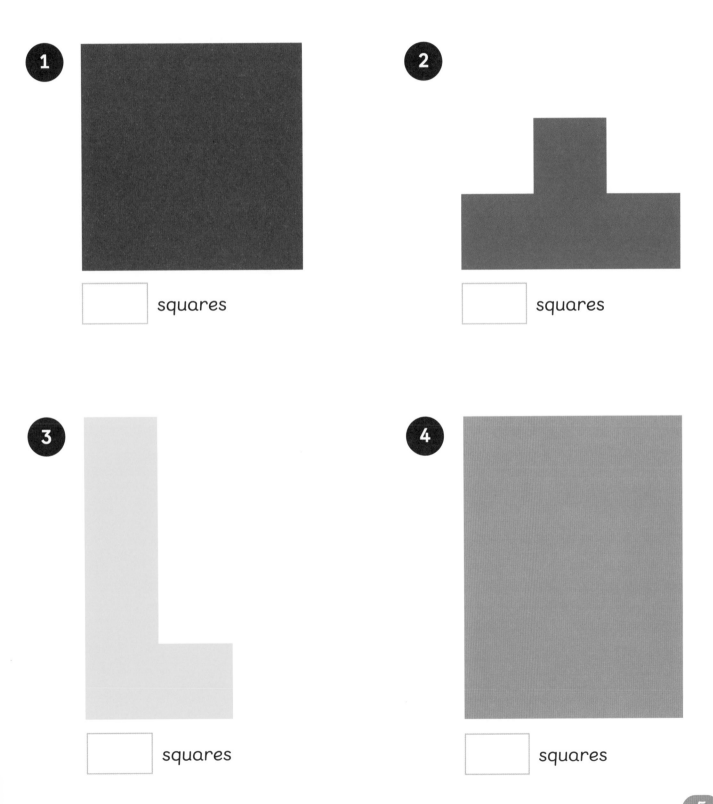

1 ⬛

[   ] squares

2

[   ] squares

3

[   ] squares

4

[   ] squares

Measuring area by counting squares

Starter

Hannah and Elliott make shapes by matching up the sides of these paper squares exactly.
What shapes can they make?

Example

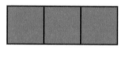

I made these shapes. The area of each shape is 3 squares.

I made these shapes. Each shape has an area of 4 squares.

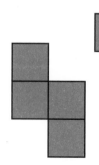

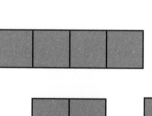

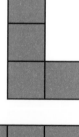

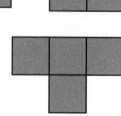

6

1 Cut out 5 identical squares and arrange them in different ways with the sides touching.
Draw some of the shapes you make in the space below.

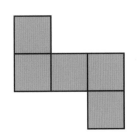

I made this one.

How many different shapes can you make that have an

area of 5 squares?

2 Circle the shapes that have an area of 6 squares.

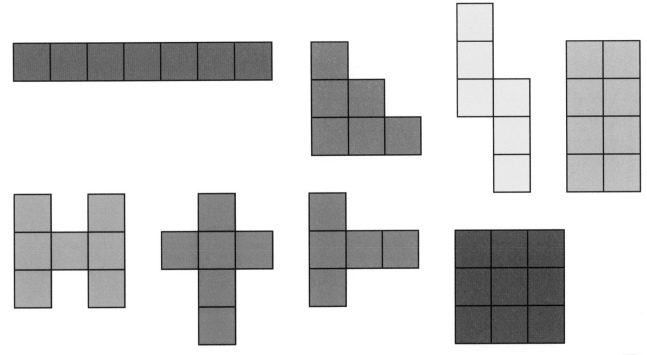

Measuring area and perimeter

Starter

Is it possible to have two figures with the same area but different perimeters?

Or two figures with the same perimeter but different areas?

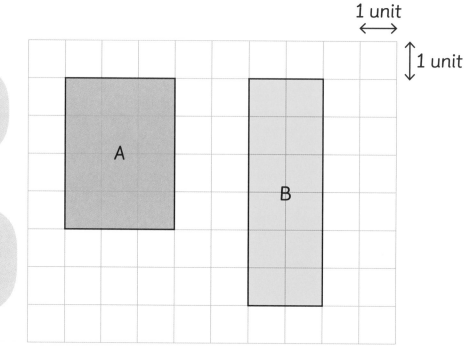

1 unit

1 unit

Example

Find the area and perimeter of A and B.

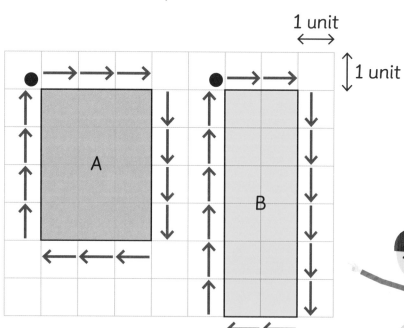

1 unit

1 unit

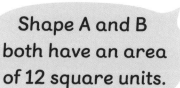

This ▢ shows 1 square unit.

Shape A and B both have an area of 12 square units.

Measure the length of the sides to find the perimeter.

Shape A has a perimeter of 14 units and shape B has a perimeter of 16 units.

It is possible for two figures to have the same area but different perimeters.

Find the area and perimeter of C.

The perimeters of A and C are equal.

The areas of A and C are different.

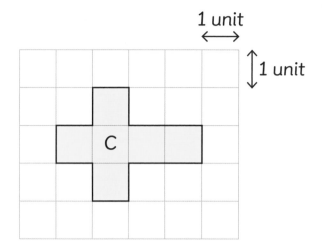

1 unit

1 unit

C

It is also possible to have two figures with the same perimeter but different areas.

Practice

1 Draw two figures with a perimeter of 18 units that have different areas.

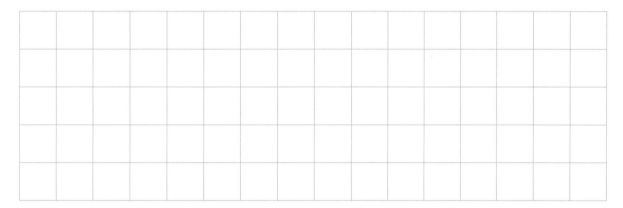

2 Draw two figures that both have an area of 20 square units but different perimeters.

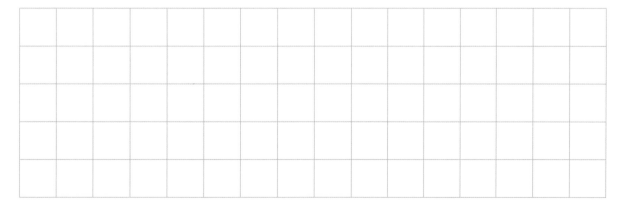

Measuring area by multiplying

Starter

Is it possible to find the area of a rectangle without counting all the squares?

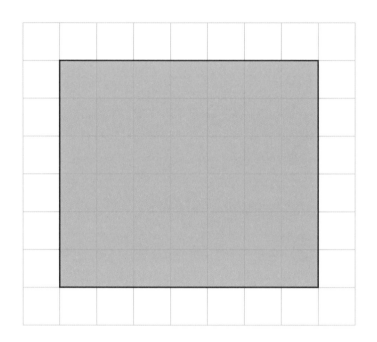

Example

There are 7 squares in a row.

There are 6 rows.

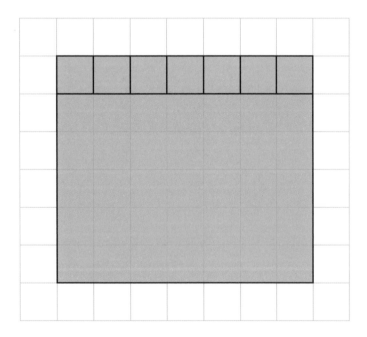

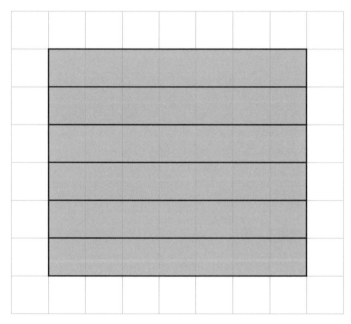

$7 \times 6 = 42$

The rectangle has an area of 42 square units.

1 Find the area of these rectangles.

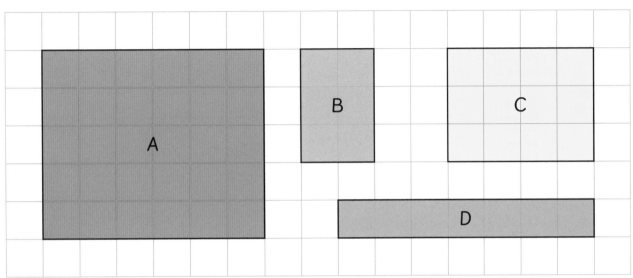

(a) The area of A is ☐ square units.

(b) The area of B is ☐ square units.

(c) The area of C is ☐ square units.

(d) The area of D is ☐ square units.

2 Draw 2 different rectangles that both have an area of 24 square units.

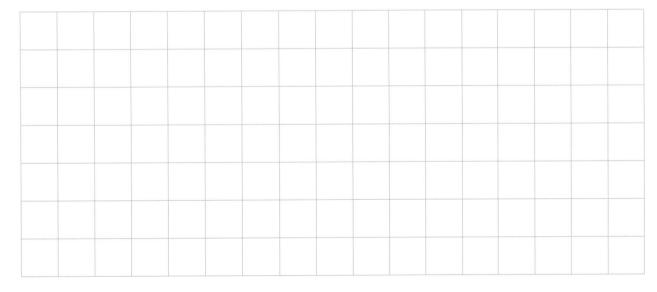

Measuring area using squares and triangles

Starter

How can we find the area of this shape?

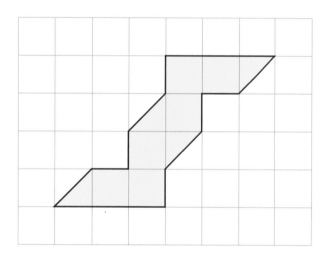

Can we find the area by counting?

Example

There are 6 squares and 4 triangles.
6 squares = 6 square units.

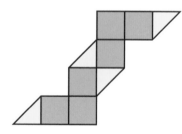

These 2 triangles have the same area as 1 square.

6 + 2 = 8
The shape has an area of 8 square units.

The 4 triangles have an area of 2 square units.

12

Find the area of these shapes.

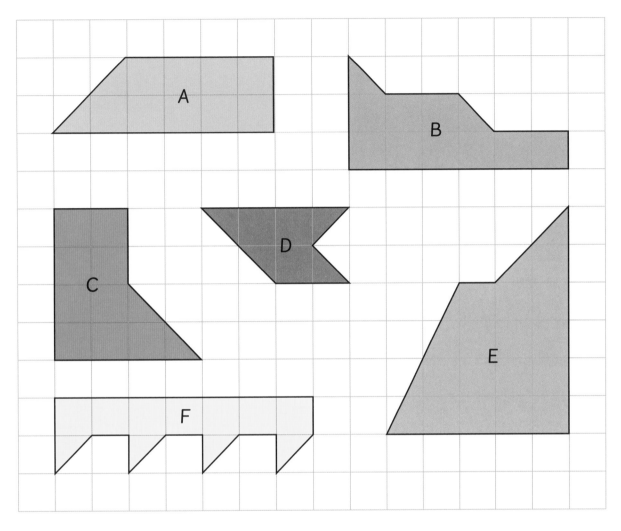

1 The area of A is ⬜ square units.

2 The area of B is ⬜ square units.

3 The area of C is ⬜ square units.

4 The area of D is ⬜ square units.

5 The area of E is ⬜ square units.

6 The area of F is ⬜ square units.

Measuring area using grid lines

Starter

How can we find the area of this shape?

 Can we count the squares?

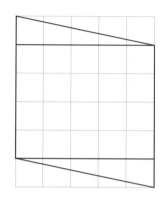

Example

We can't just count the squares.

 I can see a rectangle within the figure.

The area of the rectangle is 20 square units.

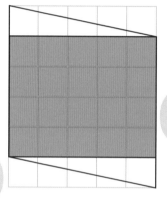

We can draw lines to show the rectangle.

 There are 2 triangles in the figure.

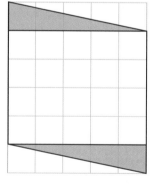

 The 2 triangles can form a rectangle.

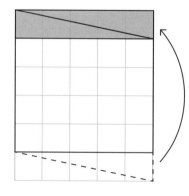

The rectangle has an area of 5 square units.

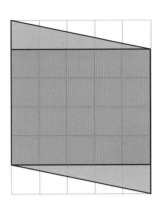

20 square units + 5 square units
= 25 square units

The area of the shape is 25 square units.

Find the areas of these shapes.

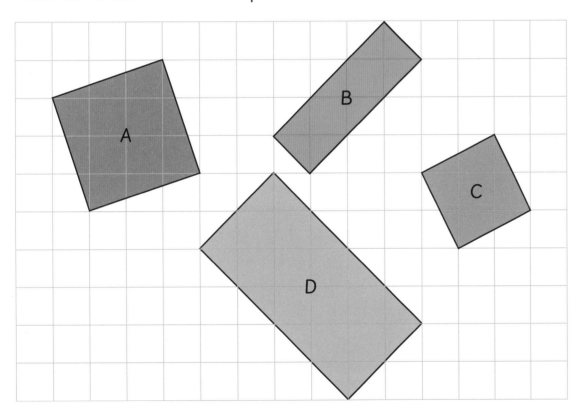

1 A = [＿＿＿] square units

2 B = [＿＿＿] square units

3 C = [＿＿＿] square units

4 D = [＿＿＿] square units

Knowing types of angles

How can we describe the different angles in these shapes?

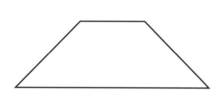

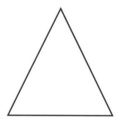

We can use the corner of a card or a book to check for a right angle.

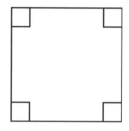

This is a square. All the angles are **right angles**. Lines that make a right angle are perpendicular to each other.

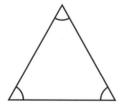

All the angles in this triangle are less than a right angle. They are all **acute angles**.

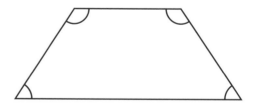

This trapezium has two acute angles and two **obtuse angles**. Obtuse angles are larger than right angles.

1 Use the corner of a card or a book to help you identify the different angles. Use **a** for acute angles, **o** for obtuse angles and **r** for right angles.

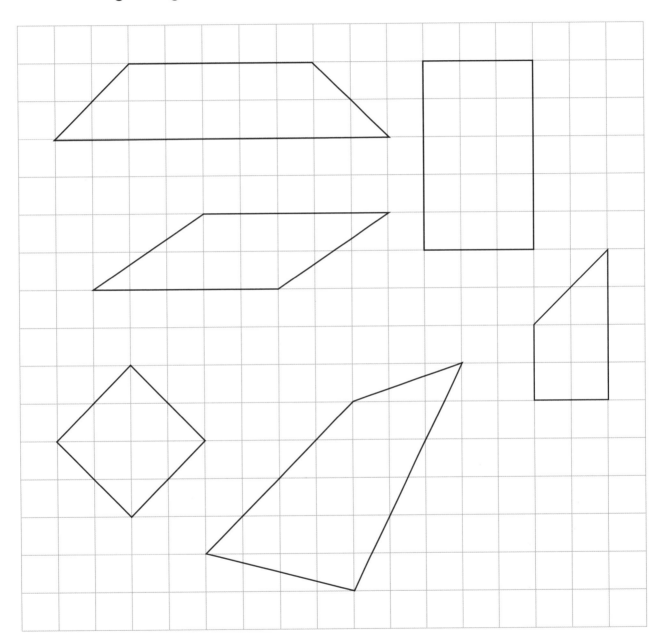

Comparing angles

Starter

How can we compare these angles?

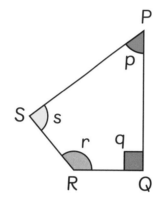

Which angle is smaller, s or p?

Example

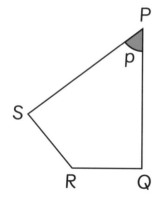

Angle p is an acute angle.
It is smaller than a right angle.

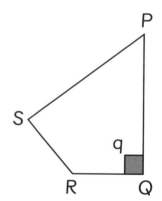

Angle q is a right angle.

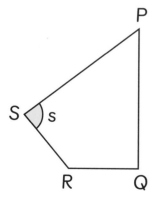

Angle s is an acute angle.

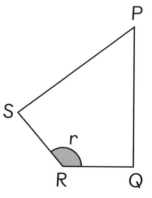

Angle r is an obtuse angle.

Angle p is smaller than angle s.

angle p, angle s, angle q, angle r

smallest   ——————→   greatest

1 Use > or < to fill in the blanks.

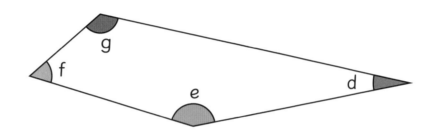

(a) angle d [ ] angle e

(b) angle g [ ] angle f

(c) angle d [ ] angle f

2 Order the angles from greatest to smallest.

angle [ ] , angle [ ] , angle [ ] , angle [ ]

Classifying triangles

Starter

How can we describe these different triangles?

A

B

C

D

Example

A

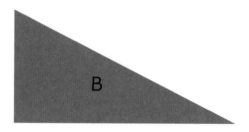

B

Triangle A is called an **equilateral** triangle because all the sides are the same length.

Triangle B has one right angle. It is called a **right-angled** triangle.

All the angles in triangle A are the same.

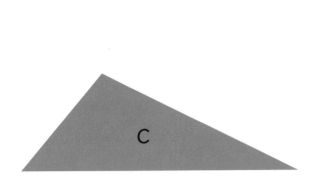

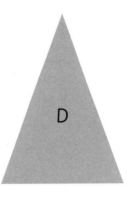

Triangle C is called a **scalene** triangle. All the sides are different lengths.

Triangle D has two equal sides. It is called an **isosceles** triangle.

All the angles in triangle C are different.

Practice

1 Label the right-angled triangles **R**.

2 Label the equilateral triangles **E**.

3 Label the isosceles triangles **I**.

4 Label the scalene triangles **S**.

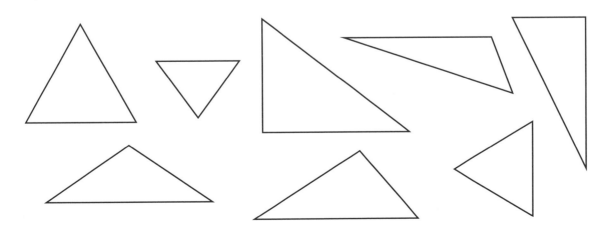

Classifying quadrilaterals

All these shapes are quadrilaterals.

What other names do these shapes have?

Example

These shapes are called **quadrilaterals** because they have four sides and four vertices.

A quadrilateral with at least one pair of parallel lines is called a **trapezium**.

This trapezium has two pairs of parallel lines. It is called a **parallelogram**.

All the sides of this parallelogram are the same length. It is called a **rhombus**.

 A quadrilateral that has four right angles is called a **rectangle**. A rectangle is also a parallelogram.

 All the sides of this rectangle are equal. It is called a **square**.

A square is also a trapezium, a parallelogram, a rhombus and a rectangle!

All these shapes have more than one name.

Practice

Label the quadrilaterals in the correct order.

1   Label all the squares **1**.

2   Label the remaining rectangles **2**.

3   Label the remaining rhombi **3**.

4   Label the remaining parallelograms **4**.

5   Label the remaining trapeziums **5**.

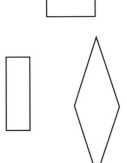

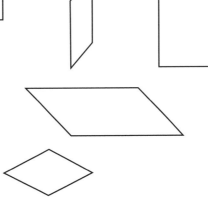
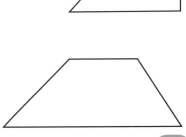

Identifying symmetrical figures

Starter

How many lines of symmetry do these rectangles have?

Example

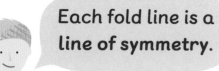
Each fold line is a line of symmetry.

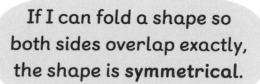
If I can fold a shape so both sides overlap exactly, the shape is **symmetrical**.

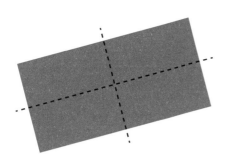

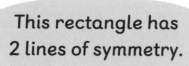
This rectangle has 2 lines of symmetry.

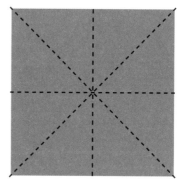

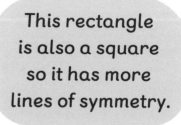
This rectangle is also a square so it has more lines of symmetry.

1 Circle the symmetrical figures.

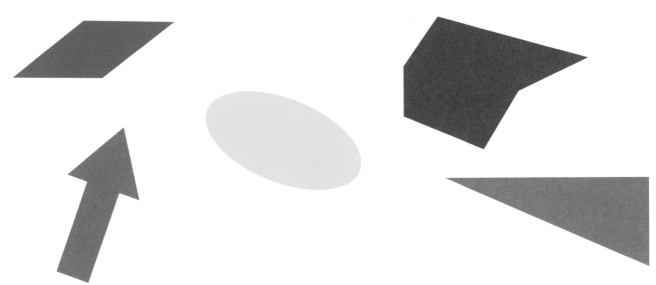

2 How many lines of symmetry do these shapes have?

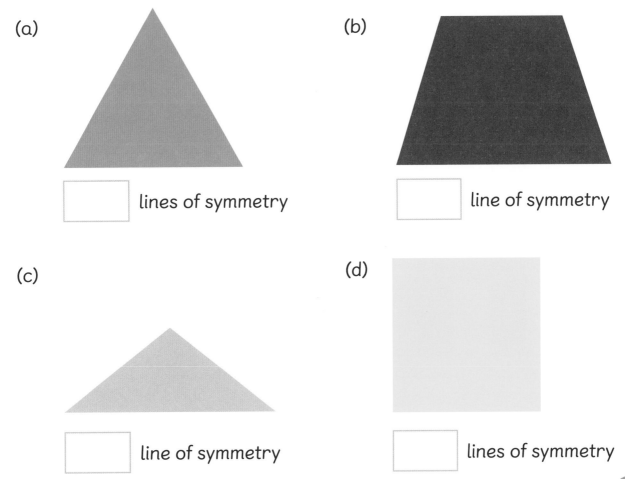

(a)

☐ lines of symmetry

(b)

☐ line of symmetry

(c)

☐ line of symmetry

(d)

☐ lines of symmetry

Drawing lines of symmetry

Starter

This shape looks like the letter H.
Is this shape symmetrical?

I think there are other shapes that look like letters which are symmetrical too.

Example

This shape has 2 lines of symmetry.

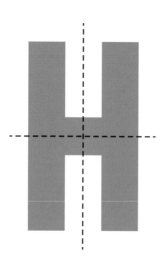

If we folded the shape here the two sides would look different.

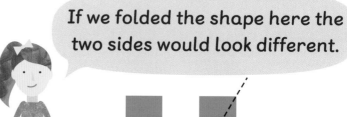

1 Draw the lines of symmetry on these shapes.

X B O
M Y

2 Draw a triangle that has 3 lines of symmetry.

3 Draw a quadrilateral with only 1 line of symmetry.

Making symmetrical figures

How can Oak make a picture of a symmetrical butterfly?

Example

Oak paints half of the butterfly.

Then she folds the paper over along the dotted line to make a symmetrical butterfly.

1 Complete the drawing to make it symmetrical.

2 Draw where the new paint marks would be if the pieces of paper were folded along the lines shown.

(a)

(b)

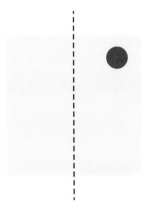

(c)

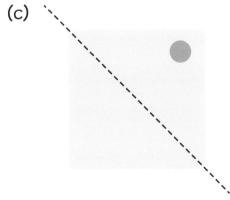

(d)

Completing symmetrical figures

Starter

Create a symmetrical shape by adding squares and triangles.

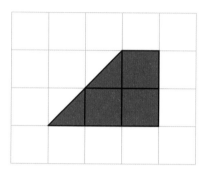

Example

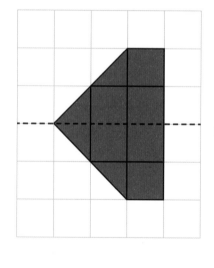

We call this the line of symmetry.

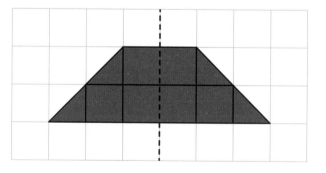

Here is the line of symmetry on this shape.

30

Make two different symmetrical figures from each shape.

1

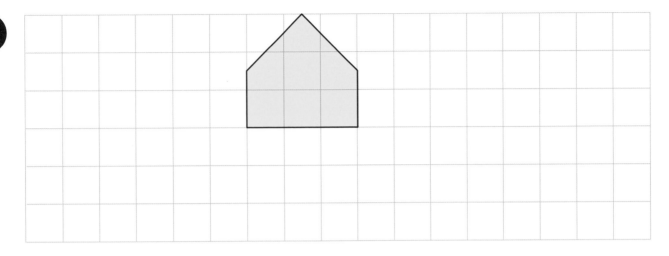

2

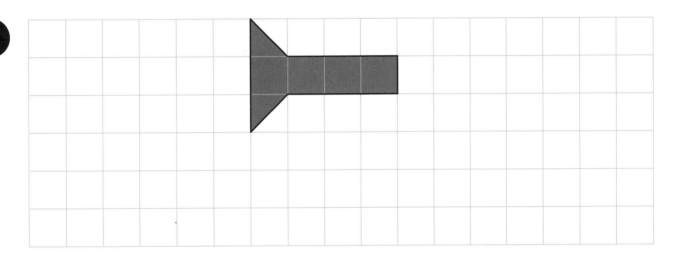

3

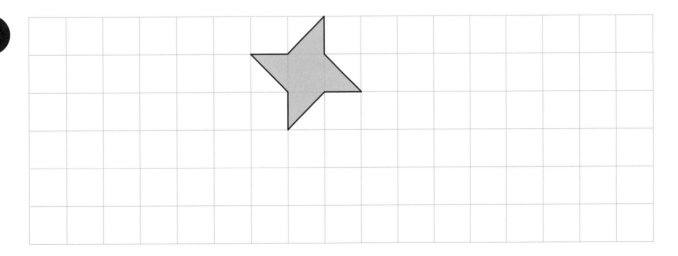

Describing position on a 2D grid

Starter

Ravi and Lulu are playing a game.
Lulu has to find the position of Ravi's
counter from his description.
What might he say?

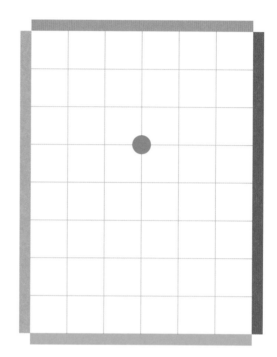

Example

Start at the
corner of the orange
and blue walls.

Move 3 units away
from the blue wall.

Move 5 units away
from the orange wall.

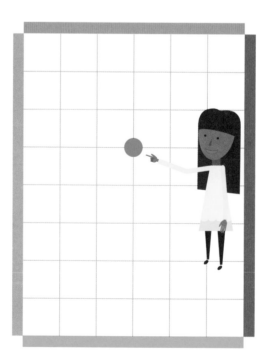

1   Mark these positions on the grid with a cross.

(a)   2 units from the blue wall and 3 units from the orange wall.

(b)   2 units from the blue wall and 6 units from the orange wall.

(c)   1 unit from the purple wall and 3 units from the orange wall.

(d)   1 unit from the purple wall and 2 units from the pink wall.

2   Join up the crosses. What shape have you made?

The shape is a [   ] .

Describing position using coordinates

How can we use perpendicular
lines to describe the position
of a point?

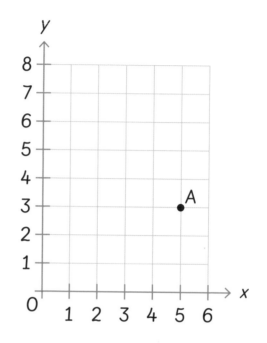

Example

We call the red line the x-axis and the green line the y-axis.

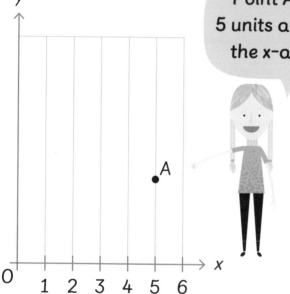

Point A is
5 units along
the x-axis.

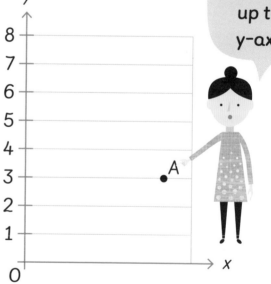

Point A
is 3 units
up the
y-axis.

We write this as (5,3).
These are the **coordinates** of point A.

1 Find the coordinates of these points.

(a) A = ([ ] , [ ])

(b) B = ([ ] , [ ])

(c) C = ([ ] , [ ])

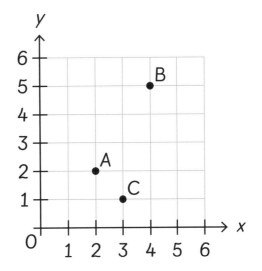

2 (a) Mark these coordinates on the grid.

P is at (1,5).

Q is at (1,1).

R is at (5,1).

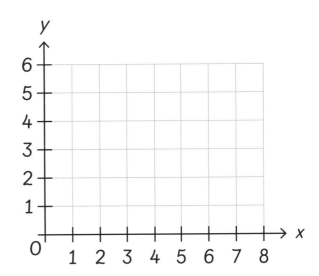

(b) Join up the three points. What shape have you made?

PQR is a [ ] .

Plotting points

Starter

If ABCD is a rectangle, what are the coordinates of point D?

What other types of quadrilateral can be made?

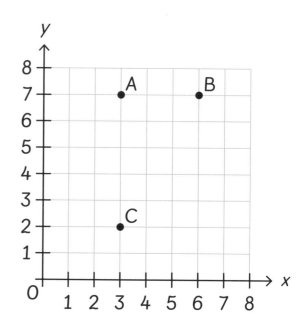

Example

ABCD is a rectangle with sides of 3 units and 5 units.

Point D is at (6,2).

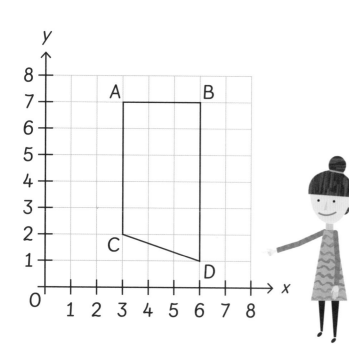

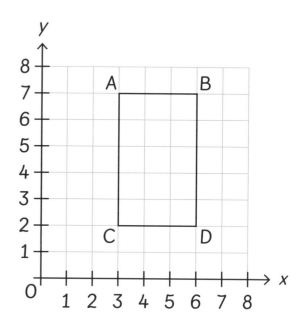

I can make a trapezium with D at (6,1).

I can make a parallelogram with D at (0,2).

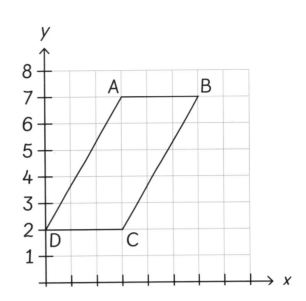

Practice

Plot these points and name the shapes that are made.

1 A (1,1), B (1,4), C (5,1)   ABC is a [   ] triangle.

2 D (6,3), E (6,7), F (10,5)   DEF is a [   ] triangle.

3 P (1,6), Q (0,9), R (6,6), S (5,9)   PQRS is a [   ].

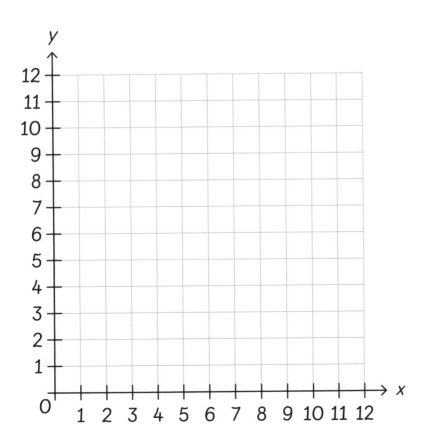

Describing position after translation

How can we describe how to get from one point to another?

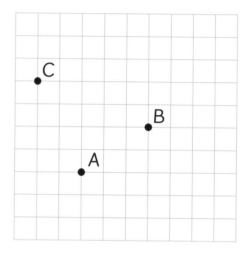

From A to B is a move of 3 units to the right and 2 units up.

From B to C is a move of 5 units to the left and 2 units up.

From C to A is a move of 2 units to the right and 4 units down.

We call this move a translation.

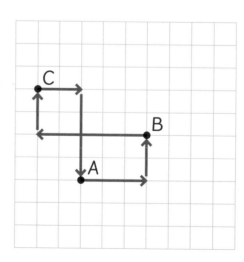

Describe the following translations using right, left, up and down.

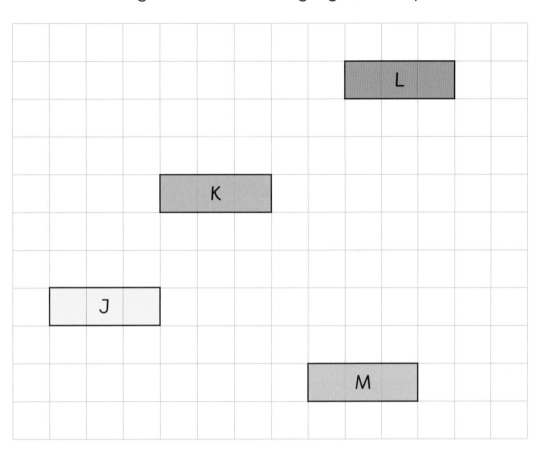

1 From shape K to shape L is a move of [   ] units to the

[   ] and [   ] units [   ] .

2 From shape K to shape M is a move of [   ] units to the

[   ] and [   ] units [   ] .

3 From shape M to shape J is a move of [   ] units to the

[   ] and [   ] units [   ] .

4 From shape J to shape L is a move of [   ] units to the

[   ] and [   ] units [   ] .

Describing movement

Describe the translation that will move point B onto (1,1).

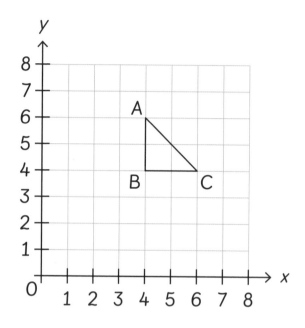

Point B has moved 3 units to the left and 3 units down.

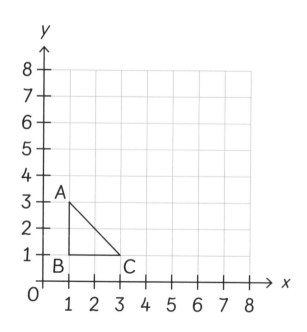

1 Draw the position of the red figure after each translation.
Use the current position as the starting point each time.

(a) 4 units to the right.

(b) 2 units down.

(c) 2 units to the right and 2 units up.

(d) 3 units to the left and 1 unit up.

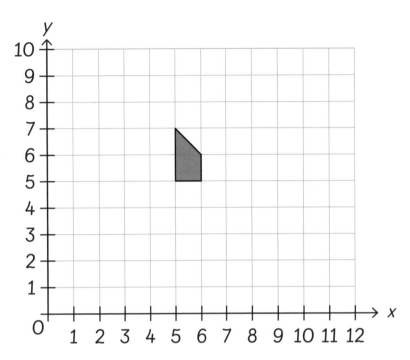

2

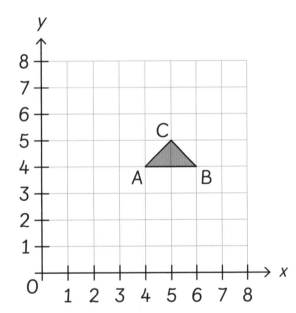

(a) Describe the translation that moves point C to (3,3).

Point C moves [ ] units to the [ ] and

[ ] units [ ] .

(b) List the new coordinates of points A and B.

A = ([ ] , [ ])   B = ([ ] , [ ])

Review and challenge

1 Give the dimensions of three different rectangles that have an area of 30 square units.

Rectangle 1 [ ] × [ ]   Rectangle 2 [ ] × [ ]

Rectangle 3 [ ] × [ ]

2 Draw two different rectangles that both have a perimeter of 30 units.

3 (a) Arrange these angles from smallest to greatest.

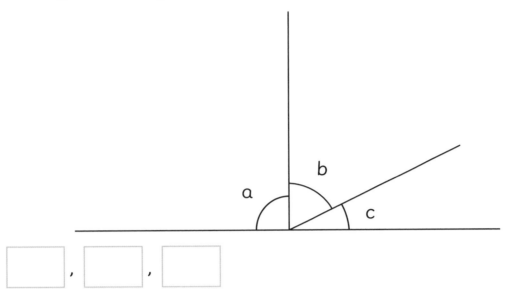

☐ , ☐ , ☐

(b) Describe each angle.

Angle a is ⬚ .

Angle b is ⬚ .

Angle c is ⬚ .

4 Circle the shapes that have 2 lines of symmetry.

H O Z W

A Y X E

5 Complete these figures to make them symmetrical.

(a)

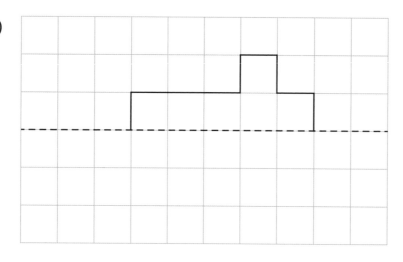

(b)

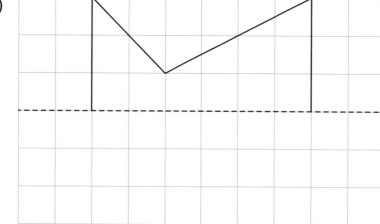

(c)

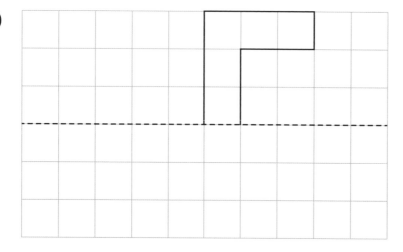

6 (a) Plot the following points and join them up on the grid below.

(2,2), (4,6), (8,2), (10,6)

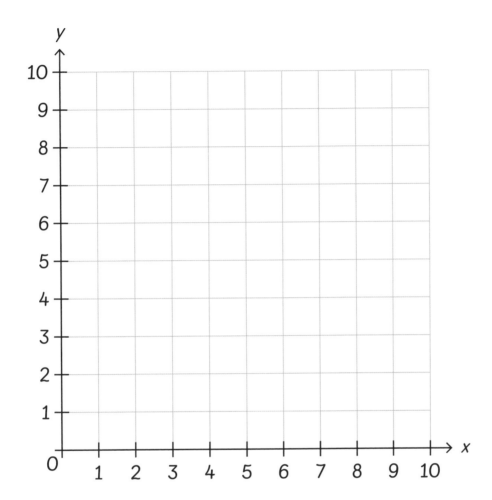

(b) What is the shape you have made?

(c) Move two of the points to make a rectangle.

(d) What are the new coordinates of the two points?

([ ] , [ ])

([ ] , [ ])

Answers

Page 5   **1** 9 squares **2** 4 squares **3** 5 squares **4** 12 squares

Page 7   **1** There are 12 possible shapes. **2**

Page 9   **1** Answers will vary. **2** Answers will vary.

Page 11   **1 (a)** The area of A is 30 square units. **(b)** The area of B is 6 square units. **(c)** The area of C is 12 square units.
(d) The area of D is 7 square units. **2** Answers will vary.

Page 13   **1** The area of A is 10 square units. **2** The area of B is 10 square units. **3** The area of C is 10 square units. **4** The area of D
is 5 square units. **5** The area of E is 18 square units. **6** The area of F is 9 square units.

Page 15   **1** A = 10 square units **2** B = 6 square units **3** C = 5 square units **4** D = 16 square units.

Page 17   **1**

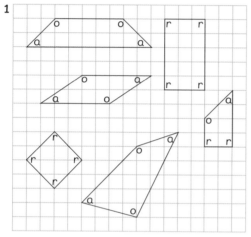

Page 19   **1 (a)** angle d < angle e **(b)** angle g > angle f **(c)** angle d < angle f **2** angle e, angle g, angle f, angle d

Page 21   **1–4**

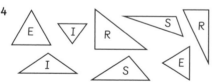

Page 23   **1–5**

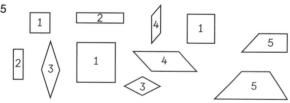

Page 25   **1**   **2 (a)** 3 lines of symmetry **(b)** 1 line of symmetry **(c)** 1 line of symmetry
(d) 4 lines of symmetry

Page 27   **1** XBOMY **2**   **3** Answers will vary. For example:

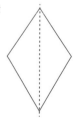

Page 29   1   2 (a)   (b)   (c)   (d)

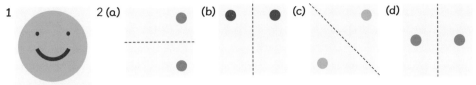
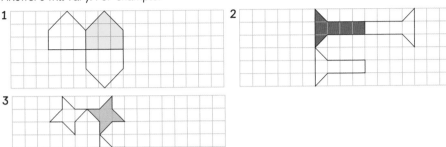

Page 31   Answers will vary. For example:

1

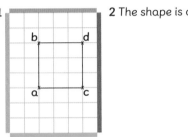

2

3

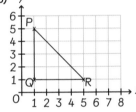

Page 33   1   2 The shape is a square.

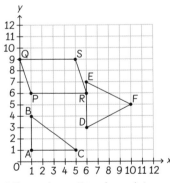

Page 35   1 (a) A = (2,2) (b) B = (4,5) (c) C = (3,1)

2 (a–b)   PQR is a right-angled triangle.

Page 37   1 ABC is a right-angled triangle.
2 DEF is an isosceles triangle.
3 PQRS is a parallelogram.

Page 39   1 From shape K to shape L is a move of 5 units to the right and 3 units up.
2 From shape K to shape M is a move of 4 units to the right and 5 units down.
3 From shape M to shape J is a move of 7 units to the left and 2 units up.
4 From shape J to shape L is a move of 8 units to the right and 6 units up.

Answers continued

Page 41 **1 (a)**

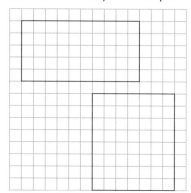

2 (a) Point C moves 2 units to the left and 2 units down.
(b) A = (2, 2), B = (4, 2)

Page 42 **1** Answers will vary. For example: 5 units × 6 units, 3 units × 10 units, 2 units × 15 units, 1 unit × 30 units
2 Answers will vary. For example:

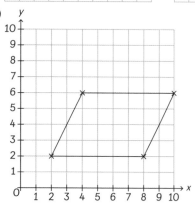

Page 43 **3 (a)** c, b, a **(b)** Angle a is a right angle. Angle b is an acute angle. Angle c is an acute angle.

4

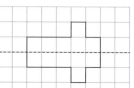

Page 44 **5 (a)**

(b)

(c)

Page 45 **6 (a)**

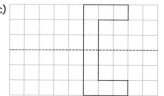

(b) a parallelogram
(c–d) Answers will vary. For example: (2,6), (8,6); (4,2), (10,2)